HAL•LEONARD
EASY INSTRUMENTAL PLAY-ALONG

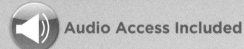

Audio Access Included

Visit **www.halleonard.com/mylibrary**

Enter Code

7074-2363-8206-3828

CLASSIC ROCK
FOR TROMBONE

T0065941

Audio Arrangements by Peter Deneff
Tracking, mixing, and mastering by BeatHouse Music

ISBN 978-1-4803-5452-4

HAL•LEONARD®
CORPORATION

7777 W. BLUEMOUND RD. P.O. BOX 13819 MILWAUKEE, WI 53213

Visit Hal Leonard Online at
www.halleonard.com

CONTENTS

4   **Another One Bites the Dust**
Queen

5   **Born to Be Wild**
Steppenwolf

6   **Brown Eyed Girl**
Van Morrison

8   **Dust in the Wind**
Kansas

7   **Every Breath You Take**
Sting

8   **Fly Like an Eagle**
Steve Miller Band

10   **I Heard It Through the Grapevine**
Marvin Gaye

11   **I Shot the Sheriff**
Eric Clapton

12   **Oye Como Va**
Santana

9   **Up Around the Bend**
Creedence Clearwater Revival

ANOTHER ONE BITES THE DUST

Words and Music by
JOHN DEACON

Steady Rock

BORN TO BE WILD

Words and Music by
MARS BONFIRE

BROWN EYED GIRL

Words and Music by
VAN MORRISON

Moderately

EVERY BREATH YOU TAKE

Words and Music by
STING

DUST IN THE WIND

Words and Music by
KERRY LIVGREN

FLY LIKE AN EAGLE

Words and Music by
STEVE MILLER

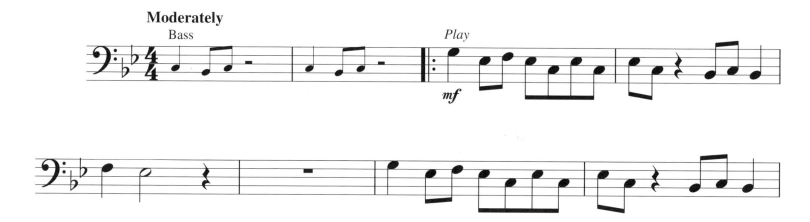

UP AROUND THE BEND

Words and Music by
JOHN FOGERTY

I HEARD IT THROUGH THE GRAPEVINE

Words and Music by NORMAN J. WHITFIELD
amd BARRETT STRONG

I SHOT THE SHERIFF

Words and Music by
BOB MARLEY

OYE COMO VA

Words and Music by
TITO PUENTE